GHETTO BLUES

Poems

Tendai Rinos Mwanaka

Mwanaka Media and Publishing Pvt Ltd,
Chitungwiza Zimbabwe
*
Creativity, Wisdom and Beauty

Publisher: *Mmap*
Mwanaka Media and Publishing Pvt Ltd
24 Svosve Road, Zengeza 1
Chitungwiza Zimbabwe
mwanaka@yahoo.com
mwanaka13@gmail.com
https://www.mmapublishing.org
www.africanbookscollective.com/publishers/mwanaka-media-and-publishing
https://facebook.com/MwanakaMediaAndPublishing/

Distributed in and outside N. America by African Books Collective
orders@africanbookscollective.com
www.africanbookscollective.com

ISBN: 978-1-77931-495-6
EAN: 9781779314956

© Tendai Rinos Mwanaka 2023

DISCLAIMER
All views expressed in this publication are those of the author and do
not necessarily reflect the views of *Mmap*.

Dedication

To those who have called home and perished in the Ghetto streets of Zimbabwe and those who were killed on August 1, 2018 Army shootings

Table of contents

Introduction

Even though Zimbabwe's ghetto musicians have been vocal in articulating the ghetto struggles through Zimdancehall music, Ghetto literature in the 21st century in Zimbabwe is an area that has scarcely got strong attention from Zimbabwean poets and writers writing now. Yes, we have tackled ghetto subjectivities and difficulties through tackling Zimbabwe's political situation, which I still do in this collection, but I also went further and tackled ghetto as "place literature", developing voices for the masses in ghettos, especially in Zimbabwe's biggest ghetto city, Chitungwiza. The ghetto is a place that changes you in ways that only blues music can manage to encapsulate and like Blues music this collection is both bitter and sweet. A few poems give insight into what shaped the poet, in poems about his birthplace in the east of Zimbabwe, on love, on race, on migration and xenophobia in South Africa.

And then as I have noted there are a number of poems that deals with the political situation in Zimbabwe, post Robert Mugabe's Zimbabwe, particularly on post-election violence of 2018 and how the entity in Harare continues to infringe on the rights of the citizens. Ghetto Blues like my previous collections, *Mad Bob Republic*, and *Revolution*, are collections of struggle poems. Ghetto Blues has 33 poems written in free flowing, informal and sometimes in prose forms.

As we head toward another election, this collection is a welcome addition to literature to do with politics, struggle, and electoral democracy and highlights social issues of the ghetto beings; issues to do with ghetto violence, religion, youth drug abuse, poverty and economic struggle, lack of social services, poor city administration, dirty, pollution and sewage etc...

Meeting him in his Religion
For Jonathan Taylor

He nods his head to the same beat as you are doing
A Yoruba drum
A Zulu drum
A Bemba drum
It's the same drum loop that has been running for centuries
The survival drum
The revival drum
The carnival drum
In the villages and ghetto towns
Same places, same people, different faces
Their skins darker, the colour of essence
Their skins browner, the colour of presence
He watches some cute girl gyrating and shaking her hips
Young men circling around her like a pack of hungry wolves
Exotic food he is too chicken-shit to taste

The Africans invented the drum ascendency
The Africans invented the song transcendence
The Africans invented the dance incendiary

And the song rumbles on....

The drum's baseline digs a left hook on his ribs
And sends him tumbling down to the ground
He thunders, "I am a drug lord...
I don't push dope, I push poetry."
This drug goes right to your heart
And those who meet me in my turf, my religion
Should know that I am a poetry drug lord!

Dawn at Chigovanyika: 29 September 2019

Walking the dusty streets,
dawn stripes its waking colours;
Naked colours, ashy grey nudity,
Grey rays, chalk greys, on sandy grain roads
Of Chigovanyika of boxes; matchbox businesses, box houses
Crammed together, inside roads like the cartographer's winded down
thoughts
What she told of this land shouldn't have been our vision
Of offish-brown, greying, cackling skins, worn out clothes
Eve's angels oiling this dirty with their butts, socks
Hands, legs, tables, chairs, stools, stalls
And the counters of cardboard boxes, goods arranged
For the early bird that doesn't catch the worms
Human effigies that look like people
The people he had seen in another world
Before he came back to this mad humans' world
Of calves ceaselessly milking their dead mothers
"4bond, 4bond, 4bond kuTown makagara"
The strength in his voice is thick with method
The taxi tout calls out to the meandering
Line that waits for 2bond "Zupco Diaries"
Tanaka Chidora jots, blogs, in his Zupco Diaries
In the inner paper and pen, the maps inside
He (the narrator has taken over) looked into his
(Tanaka) eyes and saw his own distorted reflection.
As he sits waiting, watching for the 2bond Zupco buses
This man has been here long enough to answer his own questions
"3bond, 3bond, 3bond kuTown makamira"
"Vabereki ngatiswendedzane kumashure tiende kuTown"
Packing up his taxi, to the tout there are just bricks

One on top of another, breathing in tandem
It reminds him of the taxi tout of yesteryear in Jeff Masemola street
In that world of people, the *"ihambe iMenleni"* taxi tout
Streaming from his balcony windows in a flat in Lilian Ngoyi street
But this new old town waits for him with minted coin hunger
So he takes the 4bond taxi to be in step with time
Tanaka takes the 4bond taxi to be in step with
His students waiting at that olden hilltop of learning
On the greener stripes of this minted town.

For Her You Arrested Yesterday

I am afraid if I name her
You will arrest her again
You are a street that has arrested the arrested
Arresting wisdom, arresting thoughts, arresting feelings
This refusal is for her you arrested yesterday
For holding a placard in a nameless street
You are a street that arrests its own soul
You are a street that has lost its salt

To this street unnamed, closed, broken down
How can you have a name without the soils
Without the silt that enriches the soils
Without a spirit that breathes life to the soils

To this street that arrests its spirits
All I have for you is my silent heart weeping

How can you tell the spirit not to be the breeze
That wind minds in this straight-jacketed street
Wind that whispers wisdom-coated vowels
Of women's strength, are the wind's howls
No wind holes are offered, holds sway.

To this unnamed street, desist, detract
From incarcerating the spirits for seeing
Stop putting the spirit on trial- jailing it
For without the spirit you will watch your life
Spin from the prisons of your inchoate mind
And dream of murdering the mother of your children
Before she pushes you into the Dudinka curve

Or drowning the fruits of your loins into the Darien gap
In this sea of endlessness, wilderness, wildness
Before they wield the pens to extrude you out

To a street that arrests its own spirit
Stop floating in your Magellenic camp of righteousness
And swim in the waves of your self-denial puke
A colourless soul,
humankind's stillborn bastard!

Before the Earth was smacked by a Hammer

The soul dances;
Singing songs of the flowing mountain ranges
Tying the eastern spaces to the ancient days of formation
Wind chiming memories of the warriors of the land
Knitting the gaps together in this epic offering.
Waraza, the virgin girl who sacrificed her right breast
For the rains, fertility, to allow us to live...
A woman of strength, speaking up for us to the mountains.
Nyawembera, the spirit dust that moves the rains,
Clouds, lions and python snakes
Always keeping rolling up to the skies
Wanting to be the blue of the skies.
The way smoke always prefers rising to the heavens.
The white regent Baboon of Muchena Mountains,
Seeding rain with his feet and, he walked from mountain to mountain
The fated Old Lady of kwaHogo
When she is standing she is rains in Nyanga Mountain
Standing her old pain-bones, remembering to feel nothing,
Standing with a finger pointing toward the skies of grandfathers
For a rite of passage, mending the skies with the pointing forefinger
Her feet firmly planted to the ground of grandmothers
For a link to the past,
The python spirit snake at Mouzi Mountain
Rolled into *Hari yedoro remasvikiro*
Refusing with the rains until we fill this clay pot with rain beer.
Back then we hadn't let the TV tell us to be free
To have no culture, to be who we were not.
We hadn't let the TV tell us of a god we couldn't see his teeth,
A god subjected to popular opinion.
A god who could bite you unawares
Journeying back to that time again, when there was order.

After it had rained, the open roar of Nyajezi river at paBirira falls,
The faraway monster breathings of Nyangombe River
Full of water as she sheds into Zambezi river.
As those secrets of ours left with Nyajezi river
Finding a new home in the far away vast grounded skies

Svosve, Zengeza afternoon: 20 October 2019

The old man whose heart gave up
Like the quiet that has left this ghetto's streets
As cars, bicycles, pushcarts line its edges
The old man who conquered an accident
That took his wife, children, a friend...
He has now traded ceremony for distance from us
Championing for us a winter of hot reception
The old man whom he used to joke with
Buried his name and the path he chose
He wants to dig out the dirty where the old man's seeds came to rest
He wants, he wants, he wants, to burn it
To ash and forget the laughter they had together
The old man who was his father's friend
Began to hum a tune of a trail song
Of wear and war and waste...
The wife of a friend he grew up with in these streets
Eased away from what he knew of her
His sister's boyfriend of over two decades ago
She cannot wait for time to touch her with old ways of loving
The father of his neighbour, the neighbour's mother,
Beginning with a riddle of silence
The old church girl he was friends with since she was 12
Eaten up by bp at 20, he whispers her name *Karen, Karen, Karen*....
Who said angels have white wings only?
The tens he hasn't seen since he returned from the world of people
He looks around himself to see their shadows
He looks inside himself to hear their voices,
An open mouthed roar containing secrets he cannot tell

Rivers of Despair

Eyeing for a 5kgs bag of maize flour at snaking lines, we wait
Whilst they went to the back of shops and get all they want
Eyeing a plate of Sadza and Mutowejongwe, we wait
Whilst they eat pizzas and burgers in Harare North
Eyeing for a bucket of water at Mai Getty's Well, we wait
Whilst they have dams and boreholes at their backyards
Eyeing for a $100 salary at their sweatshops, we wait
Whilst they have billions thrust into their hands by RBZ

At home electricity was cut out
Running water ran out and never ran again
Meat is the perfume we smell once a week next doors
We bite and gnaw tree bucks and roots
And the hum of crickets and bugs cool us

They go to the eateries
To heat up their spoons in soups and flavours
We ran around feeding them for a toiletries' worth grocery
Bleeding the little protein from dry vegetables, we ate,
Last night, we ate;
Tearing open a bag of *mufushwa wemunyemba*
And a small pouch of *musone weruni*
We ate it all heavy and sour with too much peanut butter

And we slept:
Slipping our bodies on reed mats and plastic blankets
The discomfort carrying our wrought bodies awake
In heavy nights of demon-wake dreams
Where demons put pies into hungry mouths

One by one, we fell down and leave for…,
5 people are standing together at this quiet place
They look at each other for strength
Hand on hand they grip each other
At that quiet place full of open-closed earths that have shed their last tears
Above the sobs, the feverish chants begin,
"Hiii hii hii, yuwii mwari woye, matisiya tiritega, hii hii yowee..."

For these are our old and our new traditions
A child will stand in the name of her people!

Huffs from my puny soul

Loneliness wakes me up from an impatient sleep.
It wakes me up on my psychiatrist couch.
Closing my mind in opening the doors of my mind.
I am old thoughts, words un-hold me.
My breathing is now speechless
The keening sound is the sound of my soul crying,
The tremours of my wounds weeping
Like the night's waves of blackness gaming my eyes.
Every middle of the night I awake to the pain screams of my mind
Lashing against the universe of my puny skull.
I endure ropes roiling my stomach and intestines into tight pain-knots.
My bone marrow squeezing my bones
Like the constricting python snakes breaking down their food
Before they swallow me whole.
My hands are bush fires,
Everything they touch turns into sooth and ash.
My teeth ache, biting with vengeance into my lips and tongue
Proselytizing their cut and paste manifest identity.
My days are broken pieces of time.
People can only touch me with their shadows.
I feel the mists of their words,
The vapour trails of their laughter.

.

Zengeza 2 Shopping Centre: 24 October 2019

The things that avoided him the last three years
Walks with him on his way to the shops
The things his eyes are seeing again
Black tarred roads, virginal coloured buildings
Soft-full bodies, sweet white smiles, chocolate skins
Replaced by sandy offish grey gravel roads
Crackling walls, soot-soiled, decaying colours
Craggy hard skeletal bodies, yellow black smiles, ivory brownish,
khakish skins
As hunger has taken a lotus position on their frames
These are the thingish humans of his world
The humus in the box houses, broken gates, doors, rotting
Windows, dry water tapes, dark bodings of no electricity
The long endless queues, *come back 2008*, the walks
With containers of water, the littering, the hunger
On their faces, hands, minds- for freedom, for food
Marching, the march in open prisons for streets
You will meet him on this ground, in these methods
In the high tide and bask of the sun
In the ebb and flow of these thingish humans
In the sides of the walkways, the wares, food...
Fish, tomatoes, veggies, fruits, foreign currency...
Books, meat, clothes, cars, humans, humans...
Hallos, call outs to the ebb of humans pouring
From every opening to the surrounding box houses
Zengeza 1, 2, 3, 4, 5 to Seke Unit A, B, C, D, G, H, J, K, L, M , N, O,
P
Numbers and alphabets names this place
To numerical St Mary's sections, Manyame Park sections, Nyatsime
sections...
And at night under the moonlight of the heat of the departed sun

In miniskirts, skimpy dresses, polished painted faces
Near the electricity place, at the new complex
Are women of the night selling their human tomatoes
To the lies that greedily satiates imagined hungers
The lies that soothes imagined horrors
To the lies that pass for people's legs
As the moon speaks in riddles
She knows, she knows, she knows, the wind it blows
The spirits in the wind weighs a million arrows her way

#ZimbabweanLivesMatter and the Villager

#ZimbabweanLivesMatter without the villager's hums
Is to say Zimbabwe is Harare, Harare is Zimbabwe
Lazily I borrow from the mad motor-mouth professor
And when the crying fades away we will realise
#ZimbabweLivesMatter was our own wounds tagging
Yesterday I woke up to sounds of social medias'
Pain screams like a fire on my mind, lashed with
#ZimbabweanLivesMatter, #Zanupfmustgo #NoToCorruption
Fighting #NoToSanctions, the twitter, the twaz, twangs, tines
In the villages they wait, weed, water and hive to homes
For the beast that comes where the sun spreads its scaly tails
Covid 19 flies our way, Covidho, iye Rona wacho; Corona Virus
Impatient death furious stalks the hatched together huts
The villagers in fear, refusing to go with this beast
I rub the sun dry bones of resistance in mushamukuru
#ZimbabweanLivesMatter in Zimbabwe's biggest village
Bracing for poverty, hunger, disease- death stalks me
My life matters, #IAmAZimbabweanToo
My opinions matters, #IAmAZimbabweanToo
Break the divide, dive in, reach out, touch, teach
#ZimbabweanLivesMatter to all the Zimbabweans
Our hope floats into the wind like soap bubbles
As dust accumulates on us, we feel the worms stirs under our skins
We shiver under our faces, wet with tears
And when the soldiers ask who shall be shackled
An answer will come to cast the chains away
I will name my unborn child: Hope
And Tariro whispers to take us home
Where we will cradle the memories lovingly

Talk is cheap

There is no truth in things, but only in humans.
Power will come from the beautiful in deeds.
True art will blossom in the flowery and fullness of humanity,
Kneaded in humility and kindness.
I use my sun dry bones of resistance as drum sticks
Chiming to the drums like remembered memory.
I want you to remember my dreams,
To be the vision that awakens from my words.
To translate me from this page and start a fire that refuses
To burn everything even though it stays alive
To know where you are by the sound of your grandmother's voice
I could have been any type of bird, doing a number of things
But I chose to be a poet
Being a Zimbabwean poet is being misunderstood
By your own mother, not wanted by your own father,
And pushed away by both.
But I will leave without my voices, a goddess defeated by time.
A cemetery of artifacts,
The evolving thing that gets used but never depletes.

When the Streets are always Policemen

In the political volcanoes of our time
The police always fills the streets with button sticks,
Ak47s, for cleaning, clearing the human rubble;
The nurse holding placards of her poverty
The teachers breaking chalk and dust for free
The women waiting for their children to come from the schools.
The hawkers that stomp the dusty and cobbled streets everyday
The doctors, the factory workers, the suited...
Fighting for freedom without construction,
An utopia without them.
The chill of the policemen's eyes are always like the snaps of dry twigs
They have freedom dispersing bullets ready in their guns
They cut, chisel, and bore at these facts
The twisting of mouths and tongues
Crying has to be unlearned.
By the cry thing caught in this swirl of dying.
Dripping with sweat and blood.
The scattered remains of disobedience.
In blood, decorating roads where names become heroes.
As the ghetto houses absorb the scurrying street passengers
And tears clean the walls of these ghetto rooms
Like Mary's tears on the cross.
They slow down these silent sounds of drowning.
In inner horizons that are blurred with painful silence.
Still sensing the stillness yet to come.

A Poem For The Present Grief

Grief is a wave before sound
That ploc of unknown, across time, ahead of time
Beyond the simple past tense into remote time
Becoming the human in humanoid humans
The humans coming and they will feel this way too

He had been going down the mountain for a long time
Going around and beyond his time like the feeling ways
Closer and far away each time to the end of the beginnings
The old man comes closer and he hears *you are here,* his voice
The old man knows he should be the last ones
He can't wait for it to touch him with old ways of seeing
The dying light in his voice is thick with human noises
He is the fire to the voices of his forefathers

The splurges of the universe retracts and reconsiders
Each highland glows tinier, higher and heavier
The walls that force things into secret ways grows
Explanations turn upon themselves into: *I am here,* his voice-
Am I revealing anything about myself, he asks himself?
I can't pretend to be myself, he thinks!
Definitions turn into themselves in, *you are here,* not his voice-
He can't pretend to bury his uncles and chose a path
Ease away from what he knows of himself

He had promised as much never to utter their names
In the miscued guttural tongue of his uncles
How they had them outnumbered with guns, dogs and bullets
In the eerie noises of the guns the old man sees again the wanton
waste
That comes with a killing field, feeling their screams

17

The butchering noise consumes the ghetto streets
As mothers gather their children's bones to make necklaces to
strangle themselves in
Whilst the milk of their vanities seeps into the thirsty ground
The car horns, the hawkers howling, the kids' last hark and cry
The people moving all over, falling down, gutted.., one by one
And the stray dogs unearthing their heads out of the street bins
And bolt away into the nearby forests
In the dusty cloud chases from the fattened handled dogs
Like wind his hair becomes screaming horses
The howls of thundering hoofs and angry neighs

Declaring his next battle on the images of these killings
The old man let his life book fall into the Well of dreams
And place his lips on the floor of hell
But the voices still comes up from the Well
Silence is a mangled body of this noise
The wails comes up from their voices
Only the effort to articulate the voices now matters
The voices comes up from the Well
Every word feeds lost and lonely spirits departed
The voices are now freer underground
Than they were overground
Death is now living in leaving, in freedom
In red blossoms belching a song of legendary strength

When it happened is best pronounced in a glottal voice
Of when it happened
Ythawc thauw thein twack thewn whitr thohn

The sticks and stones that shaped us

The tall anger you didn't want to pass through at that first platoon they called Nyatate primary school, singing, *"VaNyamavhuvhu* (Mr Nyamavhuvhu, accruing the 8th month to himself) *in'anga* (is a witchdoctor) *vanoshopera* (he foretells) *vakabata choko* (whilst holding a chalk), *teerera unzwe* (Listen and you will learn)" to his angry war cry before he baptizes you with stoned fists. The touch of this witchdoctor's bones off the ground always signaling impending ritual of stoned fists. *Kutonhodzwa kwaMambo Chauruku* (The Silencing of King Chauruka, not as in the novel) would rage with anger that could only hurt us. And our parents conniving with Chauruka's anger, telling us this was good for us. How could that have been for our good, since we were not King Chaitezvi? *Manyore ngenzeve* (Mr Manyore, the ear twister), will squeeze and twist your ears until they start picking up the sound waves of Radio 2, they now call it Radio Zimbabwe. Oh, you will hear *Ezomgidho, Madirativhange, Dzakapombonoka* in your *Radiohead* ears. Afterwards he would tell us it hurts him more than it does us. How could that have hurt him more? Mr Marabada "Bend Down My boy" the leader of this first platoon, leading us to his office between grade Six A and Grade Seven A classes like prisoners of war, where our buttocks would face him as his sticks accompany his "bend down my boy", "bend down my boy" and *"Nyama marabada", "Nyama marabada"* satisfied chants, enjoying his super beef meal. How did that hurt him more than our buttocks that would develop several throbbing heartbeats? The strength in his voice thick with anger, Mangwende making us belt his war cry, *"Ticha wedu watinaye pano* (our teacher we have here), *ndiye waMangwande* (he is Mr Mangwende), *vane basa guru* (he has an important job)", to beat the hell out of us! *"Tikafamba* (we will walk), *tikakwire makomo*

19

(we will climb mountains), *takarara panzira* (we will sleep in the middle of the journey), *kwaMangwende kure* (Mangwende area is far) into Mashonaland's flowing veldts as we became the things that natured his hate. Never mind Muchirewesi' warping backhand that would throw you out of the marching line as you left the assembly, like marching marines of the first platoon. Us, always being things that nurtured his anger. And in the second platoon, a cluster of buildings over the small knoll, was Nyatate Secondary School, "engineered and geared by Tsara, the man who coughs money", he would say that after dictating Political Economy notes from his head to us, confusing us with terms like bourgeoisie mode of production, ringing through our heads like Manyore ngenzeve's twisters. *Jongwe rine rhafu Makunura* (A Cock is rude, Makunura) would misname Geography, stick-totting around the classroom asking us, "What is *jiografu?*", and he only wanted to hear one answer, "geography is the study of the world globe in general". Nyakauru with his *Mipanda yeChishona* (Shona Noun Classes) forcing us to accept 20 noun classes instead of 21 because some son-in-law at curriculum development unit was ashamed of the 21st *Sva, Sve Svi...* noun class. I wanted it, everyone wanted it so I argued for the 21st amendment until he threw a blackboard duster at me, furious with me...years later I would see the blackboard duster's perforated desk as a reminder of Nyakauru's *Svi...* denial. Fucking hypocrites denying out of existence the thing they did every night! I would have forgiven them if they had said, "we don't recall the 21st noun class", "we don't recall the 21st noun class", "we don't recall the 21st noun class".... Sorry villagers and headmen of Svosve Street, you don't exist, the government said so! *Ndikakukiya unokande ndove Makwaza* (if I beat you, you will shit-piss your pants, Makwaza), and *Kitsi* (The Cat, Nyamandwe) were our second platoon commanders, and their captains in who-has-a-bigger-d..., major general Mukaronda and major general Chibvuri always quarreling against each other. And after 4 years, the 12 of us who got 5 O levels and above escaped this platoon to get into another platoon. It was the three of us who left for the third platoon, Marist Nyanga, nestling on the slopes of Nyanga Mountain, commanded by *Ngugiiiii*, we would call him our own WaThiong'o. Muzawaza, the English master, tall dark dangerous disciplinarian who is still weeding the crops high up there as the colonel in the ministry of preparing and seconding education. The younger Muzawazi, the younger Chinamasa, Chirombe, the 'hot' *Miss Crow*- we were bees hovering around the vibrancy of Miss Crew's flowers... I will leave these for another day for we are not yet dead!

The streets have swallowed them

Walking the noisy streets,
Through the little paths of the ghetto hoods of Chitungwiza,
Surrounded by dusty broken streets,
Garbage strewn on the sidewalks,
Flat board houses, broken down cars,
Mutorito (meth) gassed young men loiter
And litters the streets,
Mary J boys moving like the flight of dragonflies,
Hissing in the morning streets that are not even noon
Young man dressed in the colours of dust.
Showers can't wash it all;
Something is always going to stay behind
The school kids sniffing glue on the 8, O'clock news,
Mapping guidance into drunken lit waves.
Drunkards hovering in the evening streets
That will become their bedrooms
Soul-scoured with self-inflicted liquid whippings.
Drinking the elixir of their rotten dreams
Always in search of the drunken state
In the depth of the nights they call out
Like stray cats in winter nights of cold sweepings.
The shadows on their faces float with broken light.
And mothers have accepted failure
In curving men out of their sons.
Fathers are too busy looking for food
To think about the sons they no longer know
And my God, by Virgin Mary, do you blame them
Of being unafraid of dying,
For building shrines to all that has been subtracted from them.
This bell signal goes out to every ghetto home
In every city, town, village…

It has reached an intolerable degree.
A family of locust has found Zimbabwe.
Let us relive the second Chimurenga's last stand.
In the fourth Chimurenga war of eradicating drugs from our streets
We have to bury our hearts in this new battle of Chinhoyi.

The War for a Word

Irregardless of Covidho 19, irregardless the vaccines, irregardless of the arching lungs, the empty stomachs, we have to live through all this. Irregardless of flowers that adorn the graves, the fish, the lack of food. Irregardless the regard that bodes illness, Irregardless the word's meaning; what it was made to mean before it began to sound the way it doesn't look. Irregardless the colds of winter mornings, the smoking rivers. Irregardless of what you think I am huffing and puffing about, regard it less. Less in regard. That we, how have we allowed some committee that accepted the word, to tell us that irregardless is now an official word, officiating irregardless jaguar spot voices in the wind's mouth. What compensation accrues to those who were pummeled for illegally using the word before it became office for all? Irregardless of the pain that comes from such exclusion we regard irregardless well.

Take me home

Stones have no eyes for my feet.
I search for a wisp of what was once me.
I was so young, so messy, too busy creating chaos,
Bend on destruction.
Not knowing what to keep or to toss away.
Thus I always tossed everything out
For a long time I forgot what love was like.
Hidden behind the indivisible wall
That has kept me a stranger to myself.

I wonder and flow into dreams where flames lick the top of my head.
Day by day coming closer to it.
I peel the corner back as the mountains approaches,
Fractured stone heads like bones whitened by sand and sediment.
There is always something in me that ache for mountains.
To talk of lands filled with colour and light.
Of when light remembered instances of its absences.
An incandescent wind soothing like visitors appearing
The sun taking its mighty hike up Nyanga Mountain
Days of fog as soft a rope around my neck,
Ambling in the vales and mountain knolls like a child playing alone.
Meals melting from the vales and meadows clotted with small villages.

Waiting for the wind that could carry me
Across the sixth river into the flat country of Mashonaland.
I followed her voice over five rivers,
Her eyes misty and wet like morning dew,
Her hands as soft like cotton skins.
Wistful and cool like heaven's breath,
Soft as a thought in a dream.

My voice whispering, "please take me home".
The small O of my mouth in awe.
Any distance from her disagreeing with my unsaid thoughts
I want to be of this heaven and of this world.
To curve my image into a collection of colours
To see how the picture penetrates.

In these streets

The mothers who sell fruits and veggies in the sidewalks
Their hawker's voices competing with the smell of garbage,
Wondering if the chapped cracks of their palms
Will ever become millions or smiles.
The pushcarts, the whirling taxis,
The fume of this ghetto lifts my flesh and eats it.
I live in these ghetto streets.
I have lived at the edges of these ghetto streets.
I have walked the streets of these ghettos.
The ghetto is me in the process of being this poet.
I swallow the sewage smells and puke my despair in text.
I smell Chembere dzagunhanha (Kale) vegetables
And Sadza, cooking in the smokes of mutsatsa tree woods.
As layers and layers of poverty clothes
These unborn into nothingness.
Owning poverty like measles
These ghetto's soils still feed the feet
that have walked on top of her,
Now swallowed underneath her.

To The Infernal Gods

(I am gonna keep dancing when the light goes out)

My grandmother told me the sacrificial lambs
Give blood, sweat, tears and spirit to the sun
That will be returned back as light and life
I hear guitar strums coming from a Coldplay's song
Everyday Life, "everyone hurts, everyone cries…"
I am listening to as I pen this offering
To the Gods that hang over my happiness
I am gonna keep dancing when the light goes out

I can smell last night's *munya* warming
In the next streets' *mupangara* smokes
Enveloping me like a refused hug
From the windows, the outside world
Is closer enough not to touch it
Hunger has shattered all the walls
There is no one here to pray for me
I am gonna keep dancing when the light goes out

There is nothing more to fear in life than life itself
Tortured seams in a desert of unwashed sins
Paralyzed in a brimstone fire of lack
A spray of shrapnel litters the streets
After the huff and puff of the goaler gods
One telling us to go to the streets, one telling us the streets are off limits
Screams of betrayal frozen in the brittle cruel air
I am gonna keep dancing when the light goes out

We bear our guilt like sacrificial crosses
That we carry every day to Nyanga Mountain's top

A coward's burden we never can trade off
Those who died from this struggle
Search our souls asking us why
We left them alone to fight against these infernal gods
I am gonna keep dancing when the light goes out

Each one of us stands alone in the inside graves
Our sorrows creeps over our skins like spiders
Our souls are whipped, sour-scored by grief
Guilt is penance earned, but not paid for
Under the red glare of these demanding gods
That touch that once connected us to the departed
And connected us back to these marauding gods
Has blurred, swallowed by anger and guilt, is gone
I am gonna keep dancing when the light goes out

Old thinking stealing our tomorrows

Something happened to me when they told me a spray of bullets from Operation Dudula's rage in Joburg streets shattered my brother's heart. The grave markers' eyes were rectangular dreams rotting into dust, as we sprinkled a few drops of water on his mound and he swallowed them. Something happened to me when they told me Elvis Nyathi became the logs to the fire of their anger against foreigners into wounds that could not bleed. And no laws invented by humans can now touch him down inside the grave. Something happened to me as my brothers and sisters slip into the soils every day like years slipping away unnoticed. Basket full of bones that cross Beitbridge, still full of flesh to trade ritual for distance. Something happened to me when they told me a hit and run drunkard plowed down my girlfriend's father into the soils making me grow these thought bullets and vengeance from the cradle of her sadness as she stood alone at his grave, bearing the burden of loss alone. Something happened to me when MEC of Health Dr Phophi Ramathuba put on trial an echo of an image not yet formed for being a foreigner in a country s)he didn't yet know of. And that there is no one in this country to pray for this child but only definitions and explanations thickening like old black oil; the twitter in the air says- everyone now wants to crack Zimbabwean skulls with their dark grey claws. I call myself a citizen, a Zimbabwean, an African born here before pilgrims, but the borders call me a liar. Beitbridge is no longer a water colour line. Africa is no longer diversity but conformity. Africa is no longer unity but individual. To dream the African dream, to be like the anointed America, this is not the way to it. One's culture does not mean to hold another in contempt; diversity should breed strength

and beauty, all our hearts beating as one, same love, same hope, same song....
The true meaning of strength is in all of us

The morning I heard your father had left

The morning I heard your father had died I sat up straight on my bed- unknowingly to me you were also fighting the darkness that was surrounding you. The previous night I had talked to you of you and I curving the skies like an anti-missile destined to stop yonder spaces from destroying the cave of our hearts, when love and economy comes together. Your eyes began with a riddle of silence, you hadn't answered the distorted stillness in your eyes, but you couldn't stop looking at me. I lay awake, wide awake until the morning I was told your father had left. Crow's sorrow crept into my heart like spider' spreads, in grief we travelled across time to become humans.

Why Am I suddenly Responsible for Nelson Chamisa's Spaghetti Roads Complex: Tendai Rinos Mwanaka for Nyanga North Constituency in 2023?

So if you want me to be a politician with a religious syndrome, just look at Nelson Chamisa's preaching everyone down to the hades. The emperor Nero thinks he is a fucking African Jesus. So if you want to be in a party that talks vote rigging into winning an election, look at the MDC. Oh please! Don't ask me which MDC? Everything with that moniker, including even their front porches. Even when I had reached the near insanity of Matendadama, followed by Malema's comical theft of 100 minutes of Cereal Ramapostponer's SONA address, I am nowhere near Nero's eclectic vaulting blues; moving and flying everywhere from his village airport of Gutu North. Who cares which part of Wezhara Province the vibes are issuing from? What you need to understand is how to be under the influence of Chaunga (multitudes). And the Chihuahuas Mbiti, Jobho wemaronda, and Mwuorora barking the little boys and little girls (I mean Boy = ma(H)wende + girl = Maheremuka) into silence. Quiet, quiet, quiet enters the place… Not to talk of the Super Beer has insulted me. Cartons of super, rice, sugar (graders that level the roads every election year) allowing the super beer to transport the sugar and rice to buy back the vote. If you want me to win the Nyanga North Constituency I have to cat fight marujata Ghupa and the quiet discerning "strategic" eye of the professor Wales whose man and IDiot " Nehanda nyakasikana" Munyangagwa… the two play them like the tambourine man…. 24/7 melodic dwarf undertones.

My names

Something always happens to me when they mispronounce
my name, Tendai, the ndai as dai. My surname Mwanaka,
mwa as mau and ka as nga, tossing me into the trash heap, my
names crippled of their noises. Their effort remains though; I
can always pretend to like their efforts.

And then it is Thursday

I am free to fold down my aching back on the frazzled grey sofas to unpen this… this being a black city poem. This writes me after the rain that soaks the bones- the rains that poked fun at the dead. Please come down, be with me!

You are not you that is here. Come near me, hear me. Life is about finding order in disorder by confronting disorder. So, order it is. Plus and minus 52 thunderstorms in a week, I mean a year…, some with the destructive force of broken things. There is nowhere to go that's not slowly, I said slowly but with measured intention, subtracting its own thingness. Each short grey hair is a millennial of unribboning. Each short grey hour is a millennial of unribboning

And then it is Thursday. Everything miraculous happens a day after the midweek when people are expecting something to happen, are too happy for happiness to happen- always finding happiness. : "All I want is to be happy", says the Happy People!

Does madness ever knows its own face…, as its face keeps on repeating itself. This has nothing to do with neither repeating itself nor retelling it. In retelling we unleash so recklessly the intent that was never meant. We wield one thing and think of another like a reverse river flowing upon itself. Please come down now.

It is Thursday…, after you have broken me, create me. I don't want to be discarded ashes into the rains. If you want to be with me, let me let you ooze red blossoms at the seams for a while. Let me let you burn to ashes, that I don't want to be.

Out of the ashes, some say man raised god, or god raised man- It's the same story! Let me strangle your throat until the last breath drips out of you and I will still keep my hands near you for the sake of more red blossoms- oozing... For oozing is a newfound land that zings for me. Let me cuff you to my thunderstorms, brooding dark fangs. Yes, I feel bad for the moon.

The faint moon apologizing for my insanity to the clouds invading your inner spaces. Please come down, be with me. And let me either escape or overwhelm you with these two demons of love, both are jailing tyranny of my presence and or absence in your life. If you don't let up, I won't let you be with me.

By the way, I always choose Escape.

And then it is Thursday.

It takes a while

It takes a while to debunk that lie that there is nothing else to fear in life than dying alone. FYI, everyone dies alone, in most cases anyway. The only thing to fear is to die and leave them alone. That's the only failure in life. It takes a while to respond to the call of our hearts and when we do, we should simply follow our own footsteps into passable paths...

I am a poet of ministry

I understand the letters Mr. at the beginning of my name
Mwanaka, does not weigh enough to tip the scales
On leaders without followers sitting in hotel galleries
And the policeman's gun that is ever pointed at us
Lurking like panthers in our militarized streets
Blinding us with bullets like sunlight on mirrors

I wonder and dream phantasm, the partitioning of our city streets
"Go back, you have no permit to go this way, or that way- there"
The wide bass of Human River is jailed in boxed streets

Life in Zimbabwe is as hot as a stroke of lightning
A monstrosity crafted by the dreams of Mnangagwa's steel gaze
Condescending mind that kisses his mouth like sweat on fingers
A government intrusive, invading computer spaces
Declaring war on citizens for being Zimbabweans
Calling citizens "terrorists", promising to extinguish us
Harking his anger back to the cockroach speech of Gukurahundi
An instant that time cannot still fathom

We are more voodooed dancers entranced to the deer dancers
As we listen to the deer senators and MPidiots barking like dogs
The carnal politicos and juridical hubris as unforgiving as time
That refused to unwound this sun of thousand times over
But we still throw stones to this sun to keep alive
For in Zimbabwe the sun is all about human life or death

Day by day we push dusk into dawn, dawn into dusk
Praying for long hours away from the chainsaws
So that we can remind the next fathers of a falling nation
And our grandchildren, the fathers ahead of us

That we wished to ride in Zimbabwe until Zimbabwe is Zimbabwe
For this legacy in foreign lands is just a hunger for home

We scribble the words "human rights" with indelible ink
Dark ink intended for this patrilineal political architecture
Filled with so many Mutsatsa tree coffins, full of human bones

Give us our precious human rights
The violence in this pen is the violence of the tongue
I am a poet of ministry
Longing for a spoonful of liberty
To tell these jailors to fuck off
So that we can go and pursue our own happiness

Instead we grovel and apologize for our freedoms
With human tears still remaining of images of freedom writers
Locked in cell blocks, legs strangled in leg irons
And our freedoms slipping away as a generation of writers
Waiting patiently, watching our pens run dry of words
All eroding away in this volcano of social distance time
Making our lives heavy as a promise unfulfilled.

Praying to a god they don't believe in

Every winter always descending to bury them in lies is a god that tells them medicines are evil. Power for power they live in churches that always get the first dibs at every disease: cholera, typhoid, covid 19, small pox, diphtheria, scarlet fever, whooping cough, measles…. Always in white, the white angels of death, our streets are now infested by church after church and yet the soil always maintained its own religious quirks. There are fools at who they are, not what they do with it.

Here, Now

To this here
To this now
This kind of here
(Go and pray about it), if you want…
Murmurs
The theories it feeds upon.

And this now
(Go and argue about it), if you want…
Is an incomplete renovation.

1 Corinthians 13 vs 11-12

11. When I was younger, and to erase myself from blame, I would forget or lie, forget or lie, forget or lie... I would lie about my name, about my birthmarks, about my shadows. Forgetting would take over my name to recover what name was hidden inside my own. And when I was a teen, and to erase myself from blame, I would make strangers uncomfortable, I would make old people uncomfortable, I would make my parents uncomfortable, and then overcompensate by hugging them, that giddy feeling of power and burden was like when my first lover curved her tastes into me, combing for me the paths to new homes. But when I became a man I put away the *Tena koe e Meri* that was sung like a private anthem. Now there is still more tea to be drunk!

12. For now we see the windowed rivers, and face to face they frighten us enough. Now I know in part, it's that time to speak of love again, but then I also know that someone has to stand around and watch the cattle all day....

I never saw them again!

Somewhere in the quiet violence of the 1990s, there was this group of Watch Tower Bible road preachers, a middle aged man, a pretty slip of a girl, and the vocal young man who I used to have rousing bible discussions with every Saturday. At the end of the discussion I would give them bananas, sometimes apples, or whatever, to eat. And reliable like an assuming hour hand, the next Saturday around 8 am in the morning they will be entering my gates. I had tolerated them first time because I thought I could get inroads with the pretty girl. First days I would ask good questions to their readings and explanations. We would argue, read the bible, promise to do that next Saturday, promise each other heaven and I would give them bananas… I think the middle aged man liked me. Not that way, please! Then when I realized I could never get a moment with the pretty girl, when I was bored by their intent to try to convert me, one Saturday I decided to ask non-controversial questions when they asked me to ask questions. I am like holding their non-controversial booklets of clichés, where lions and little kids are pictured playing together in heaven, everything is the green of Uganda, the bananas, oranges, berries, cows sleeping on human beds, so I asked them what kind of paper are their sermons printed on. Who wrote the bible? Did they bind the booklets, what kind of binding, who took the cover photographs, are the staples from Germany…they couldn't say God in all the answers, and then I told them I had no bananas to give them that day. I never saw them again!

To show that an Idea has a history in order to reclaim it, by owning Miranda Mellis' Demystifications Series

#1

I am that one time when we kicked, with our bran new school shoes, that oddly shaped rock, all the way home from school. Mom looking at our broken, torn shoes with anger that could only commute with sticks, and us standing far away enough, ready to fly away.

#2

I am that Christmas day when we left the cattle in the bushes and went to the local shops to celebrate with others, only to fail to find our cattle by night's fall. They had wandered away. We were the cattle that slept at the cattle kraal learning to sentence our errant selves by staying away from her sticks. We picked up small stones and turned them into soup in our mouths like that old lady of Chivi.

#3

I am the chewed scents of Harare's early mornings as a night shift Fauwcett security guard in the Kopje area of Harare, learning that night was created by an error of commission in accounting. It was just a few hours, and then it stayed for 8 more hours commissioned to act for mornings, which is night's duty.

#4

I am that 1990s Zimbabwe hustler into mining spots, into Botswana, into Mozambique, sleeping under the pounding rains, thinking the rains would stop and make a tune that I would hear again in my heart. Surely, one does not need a body in heaven, my skins still throb when I remember about the raino.

#5
I am that boy, fresh out of high school trusting nothing else but his pen, that his pen is everything, trusting in the pentametric round terrains of an Eversharp pen.

#6
After everything, after 4 years invoicing and selling cars, cars, cars, at Amtec Motors, until cars are all I thought I hear, I turned my face in the direction I still remembered was where the pen was, heading to the old beginning....

A flag as a makeshift alter.

Number 1 chancellor road has been staring at the same point for generations now and the journey forward is the journey back to the past. Before you deliberately ferment chaos for a few donor dollars, the ever clever manipulative tactics of the esoteric, a sense of purpose is what you should first cultivate. The flag is now the only thing left for you to wave, the fists have become the open palms, and the open palms have become a thrusting back and forth pointing finger. But before you tell us the blacks are failures- that black countries are failures first thank the blacks for not putting arrows in your ancestor's backs as they exterminated our grandmothers, as they curved countries out of our countries into private property. The past is etched in all of our eyes, and the old glory has spread thinner. Black is always trying to be adjacent to white to stay black. Racism has gone downstairs and we can't have the fake without the original. Half there, now we wait...

POC

I am not black
I am brown
That's what I am seeing

Am I a person of colour?
Am I a person of interest?

POC must include white colour
For white is a colour
That's what I am seeing

I would rather you call me African
That's the only identify I can't see
Yet I am comfortable with

But if you insist on calling POC
Or calling me Black, which is a colour
Or a person of interest
Then there has to be a person of no colour?

Black is black

Black is black is grey
as naming is cursing is white
as being blessed yellow is not to have a name.

Negro, please!
Let me be your heroin hero on.
Let us learn to try harder

Its people that surround you…, always,
There are people somewhere.

Beyond This Time

I am having repetitive conversations with my inner animals
Acting as if there is no human centre inside me
Animal memories like memories of grains of sands
Of how we don't remember they were once Ice Age boulders
Listening to a language that I know but do not understand
Listening to the grandmothers I have never met
To words that have imprisoned me for a lifetime
Like a grave that cannot hide from its own metaphors

We are Waraza's grandchildren: *Everything has gone wrong....*
We are children of the tropics, a fashion of hunger for legacy
The sun crushes for our skins
Every night we unbury ourselves, every morning we bury ourselves
And ignore hunger for a living
As we try to be tangent to the sun
What burns is left to burn, until forgotten
As we gain the knowledge of hunger
And put our legs down to walk home

This tangency has to be unlearned
By refusing to worship extraordinary shadows
And ordinary laughter
Spirits that harvests that which we have lost

Beyond this time...
We are waiting for the rivers
That sometimes run backward-crested
Mountain cesspools of piled up wetness
We peel a corner of it and find other rivers approaching

The moon murmuring in riddles, shivers and shines
On rivers whitish blue, their waters from the distances
Like Tupelo's culm and crop

Lies that give shelter to our imagined hungers
Are terrors that have passed for humanity?
Adding accusations like Tsikamutanda's stories
We put out a spirit plate for these terrors
For if we love life we have to learn to placate these pilgrims

And you will never be alone if you live with your hands open
To embrace those no one wants...
Beyond this time, we are waiting, we are watching for...

And you will never be alone if you live with your hands open
To embrace those no one acknowledges...
One day I shall give them back to you

And you will never be alone if you live with your hands open
To embrace those no one remembers...
And you will store in your breath their names, their hopes, their
laughter...

And you will never be alone...

Mmap New African Poets Series

If you have enjoyed *Ghetto Blues*, consider these other fine books in **New African Poets Series** from *Mwanaka Media and Publishing:*

I Threw a Star in a Wine Glass by Fethi Sassi
Best New African Poets 2017 Anthology by Tendai R Mwanaka and Daniel Da Purificacao
Logbook Written by a Drifter by Tendai Rinos Mwanaka
Mad Bob Republic: Bloodlines, Bile and a Crying Child by Tendai Rinos Mwanaka
Zimbolicious Poetry Vol 1 by Tendai R Mwanaka and Edward Dzonze
Zimbolicious Poetry Vol 2 by Tendai R Mwanaka and Edward Dzonze
Zimbolicious: An Anthology of Zimbabwean Literature and Arts, Vol 3 by Tendai Mwanaka
Under The Steel Yoke by Jabulani Mzinyathi
Fly in a Beehive by Thato Tshukudu
Bounding for Light by Richard Mbuthia
Sentiments by Jackson Matimba
Best New African Poets 2018 Anthology by Tendai R Mwanaka and Nsah Mala
Words That Matter by Gerry Sikazwe
The Ungendered by Delia Watterson
Ghetto Symphony by Mandla Mavolwane
Sky for a Foreign Bird by Fethi Sassi
A Portrait of Defiance by Tendai Rinos Mwanaka
Zimbolicious: An Anthology of Zimbabwean Literature and Arts, Vol 4 by Tendai Mwanaka and Jabulani Mzinyathi
When Escape Becomes the only Lover by Tendai R Mwanaka
ويَسهَرُ اللَّيلُ عَلَى شَفَتي...وَالغَمَام by Fethi Sassi
A Letter to the President by Mbizo Chirasha
This is not a poem by Richard Inya
Pressed flowers by John Eppel

51

Righteous Indignation by Jabulani Mzinyathi:
Blooming Cactus By Mikateko Mbambo
Rhythm of Life by Olivia Ngozi Osouha
Travellers Gather Dust and Lust by Gabriel Awuah Mainoo
Chitungwiza Mushamukuru: An Anthology from Zimbabwe's Biggest Ghetto Town by Tendai Rinos Mwanaka
Zimbolicious: An Anthology of Zimbabwean Literature and Arts, Vol 5 by Tendai Mwanaka
Because Sadness is Beautiful? by Tanaka Chidora
Of Fresh Bloom and Smoke by Abigail George
Shades of Black by Edward Dzonze
Best New African Poets 2020 Anthology by Tendai Rinos Mwanaka, Lorna Telma Zita and Balddine Moussa
This Body is an Empty Vessel by Beaton Galafa
Between Places by Tendai Rinos Mwanaka
Best New African Poets 2021 Anthology by Tendai Rinos Mwanaka, Lorna Telma Zita and Balddine Moussa
Zimbolicious: An Anthology of Zimbabwean Literature and Arts, Vol 6 by Tendai Mwanaka and Chenjerai Mhondera
A Matter of Inclusion by Chad Norman
Keeping the Sun Secret by Mariel Awendit
سِجلٌّ مَكْتوبٌ لِثَانِهِ by Tendai Rinos Mwanaka

Soon to be released
Zimbolicious: An Anthology of Zimbabwean Literature and Arts, Vol 7 by Tendai Rinos Mwanaka and Tanaka Chidora
Best New African Poets 2022 Anthology by Tendai Rinos Mwanaka and Helder Simbad
https://facebook.com/MwanakaMediaAndPublishing/

Printed in the United States
by Baker & Taylor Publisher Services